CATCH IT!

Contents

Diana Bentley

Story illustrated by
Pet Gotohda

Heinemann

Before Reading

Find out about

- Different breeds of watch dogs

Tricky words

- watch
- loud
- intruders
- sharp
- eyes

Introduce these tricky words and help the reader when they come across them later!

Text starter

Lots of dogs make good watch dogs. They have sharp eyes and sharp hearing. If they see or hear an intruder, they bark loudly.

Watch Dogs

Lots of dogs make good watch dogs.

This small dog has a loud bark.

It can watch out for intruders.

This dog makes a good watch dog.

This small dog has sharp eyes.

It can watch out for intruders.

Terriers have sharp hearing too!

This dog makes a good watch dog.

This big dog has a loud bark.

It can watch out for intruders.

This dog makes a good watch dog.

This big dog has sharp eyes and a **very** loud bark.

It is a very good watch dog.

Quiz

- What kinds of dog make good watch dogs?
- Why can small dogs make good watch dogs?

Word Detective

- **Phonic Focus:** Final phonemes

  Page 4: Find a word that ends with the phoneme 'll'.
- Page 8: Find the adjective that describes the dog's bark.
- Page 10: Find a small word inside the word 'good'.

Super Speller

Read these words:

can   has

Now try to spell them!

HA! HA! HA!

Q What goes 'tick, woof, tick, woof'?

A A watch dog.

In this story

 Bones

 The master

 Wag

 The burglar

 The postman

Introduce these tricky words and help the reader when they come across them later!

Tricky words

- burglar
- garden
- barked
- postman

Story starter

Bones is a big dog. Wag is a small dog. Bones is a very good dog but Wag is always getting into trouble. One day, Bones saw a burglar coming into the garden.

The Burglar

Bones saw a burglar
in the garden.

Bones ran at the burglar.
He barked and barked.

The burglar ran off.

The master gave Bones
a bone.

What do you think Wag will do?

Wag saw the postman in the garden.

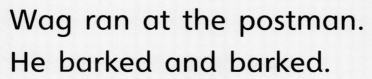

Wag ran at the postman.
He barked and barked.

"Help! Help!"
said the postman.

The master saw the postman in the garden.

"Stop! Stop!" said the master.
"Get off, Wag!"

"Bad dog, Wag," said the master.

23

Quiz

Text Detective

- Why did Wag attack the postman?
- What do you think the master will say to the postman after Wag's attack?

Word Detective

- **Phonic Focus:** Final phonemes

  Page 15: Find a word ending with the phoneme 'ff'.
- Page 22: Find the word 'stop' twice.
- Page 18: What two words make the word 'postman'?

Super Speller

Read these words:

big   man

Now try to spell them!

HA! HA! HA!

 Q What did the dog say to the burglar?

A "Stop in the name of the paw!"